FARM WORKERS UNITE

FARM WORKERS UNITE

THE GREAT GRAPE BOYCOTT

DEVELOPMENTAL STUDIES CENTER · OAKLAND, CA

First edition published 2008.

Photographs and images: Corbis Corporation. Copyright © 2001–2008 by Corbis Corporation. All visual media © by Corbis Corporation and/or its media providers. All rights reserved. (pp. 1–5, 8–10, 15–17, 19, 21, 22, 26, 27, 29, cover); Dolores Huerta Foundation, www.doloreshuerta.org (p. 13); The César E. Chávez Foundation, www.chavezfoundation.org (p. 13).

Illustrations: Rini Templeton, used by permission of the Rini Templeton Memorial Fund, www.riniart.org (pp. ii, 5, 7, 11, 15, 20, 25, 28).

Book and cover design: Nicole Hayward Design

Developmental Studies Center
2000 Embarcadero, Suite 305
Oakland, CA 94606-5300
(800) 666-7270, fax: (510) 464-3670
www.devstu.org

ISBN-13: 978-1-59892-730-6
ISBN-10: 1-59892-730-2

Printed in Mexico
  2 3 4 5 6 7 8 9 10 RRD 17 16 15 14 13 12 11 10 09

CONTENTS

STATE OF CALIFORNIA

The Central Valley and Salinas Valley of California have ideal growing conditions for hundreds of kinds of fruits and vegetables. Most of the produce eaten in America is grown in these two valleys.

SACRAMENTO

SAN FRANCISCO

CENTRAL VALLEY

SALINAS VALLEY

LOS ANGELES

SAN DIEGO

INTRODUCTION

CALIFORNIA IS HOME to the **fertile** Great Central Valley—a long, flat valley in the middle of the state. More than 350 kinds of fruit and vegetables grow there, and more than half the fresh **produce** that Americans eat comes from there.

For centuries, the Great Central Valley was divided into small farms. However, by the 1950s, most of the farmland was owned by just a few wealthy farmers. They had slowly bought land from small farmers struggling to make a living. The new farms covered thousands of acres. Grapes, strawberries, lettuce, and broccoli stretched as far as anyone could see.

To plant and harvest the crops on these huge farms, the growers needed

Migrant workers harvest peppers.

workers. Because they needed the workers only during the planting and harvesting seasons, they didn't hire permanent staff. Instead, they hired workers who moved

1

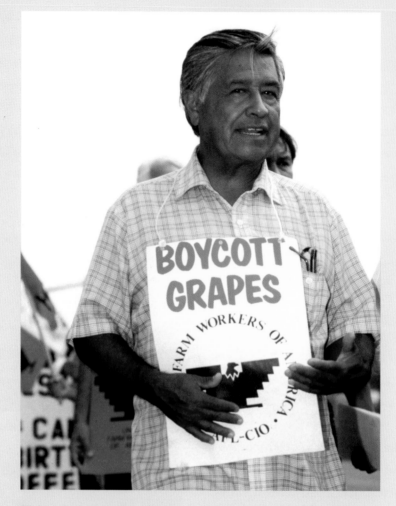

Chávez led peaceful protests such as marches and boycotts.

from one place to another looking for work, or migrant workers.

Today, about 3 million workers a year move around the United States—mostly in California—to plant and harvest fruit and vegetables. The work migrant workers do in the fields is hard, but, thanks to César Chávez and Dolores Huerta, two Mexican Americans who fought for the rights of farm workers in the southwestern United States during the 1960s and '70s, conditions for the workers are much better than they used to be. This is the story of Chávez, Huerta, and the United Farm Workers of America.

MIGRANT WORKERS

After the American Civil War ended in 1865, many migrant workers began coming to the United States. They came from countries such as Mexico, China, and the Philippines because they couldn't find work in their own countries. These people were poor and desperate for work. They believed, in the United States, that they could earn enough money to feed their families and that their children could go to school.

Since 1945, much of the farm work in the United States has been done by Mexican Americans whose families have lived in the United States for several **generations**. It is also done by Mexicans who come across the border just for the harvest season. Some come illegally. Others have papers that allow them to work legally.

Mexican Americans are often joined on the farms by African Americans, Puerto Ricans, **Filipinos**, and other workers from Central and South America.

Mexican migrant workers plant squash in North Carolina.

Mexican migrant workers pick strawberries in the Salinas Valley, California, in 1963.

1 COMPETITION FOR WORK

WHEN THERE ARE NOT enough jobs for everyone who wants them, workers have to compete for jobs. Beginning in the 1940s, migrant farm workers in the United States faced growing competition for jobs.

More migrant workers came into the United States because of the Bracero Program, which was set up by the government in 1942. Because so many men were overseas fighting in World War II, the government allowed growers to bring in extra workers (called *braceros*) from Mexico to plant and harvest crops. After the war ended in 1945, farm owners kept hiring braceros instead of other workers because the braceros

Braceros were usually paid less than migrant workers.

were willing to work longer hours for less pay. The farmers wanted to spend less money paying workers so they could keep the cost of food lower and make a bigger profit.

More workers also came into the United States by crossing the border **illegally**. Farmers hired illegal workers for the same reason they hired braceros—because they were willing to work for much lower wages than local workers. The illegal workers didn't complain because their pay was still higher than it would have been in their home countries, and they feared **deportation** if they spoke out.

At the same time the number of workers was rising, jobs were disappearing. After World War II, new machines were invented to plant and harvest crops. The machines did a lot of the work that had been done before by migrant workers. More and more farmers used machinery on their farms during the 1950s and '60s. As a result, there were fewer jobs for the growing number of workers.

2 THE LIFE OF A MIGRANT WORKER

WORKING CONDITIONS

Because there were more workers than jobs, migrant workers were easy to replace. Those who did find work knew that there were always other workers waiting to fill their jobs. Therefore, many migrant workers were willing to work in bad conditions without complaining because it was better than having no job at all.

On many farms, men, women, and children were **exploited**. They worked in the fields from dawn until late at night. There were no bathrooms in the fields, and sometimes workers weren't allowed to take breaks, even to drink water. Workers were often in the **searing** heat of the direct sun, and midday temperatures in the summer could reach over 100°F.

Migrant workers used tools that were both damaging and dangerous. The short-handled hoe, a digging tool used to thin out crops, had a handle that was only one to two feet long. Workers who used it had to spend 10 to 12 hours a day in a bent-over position. At the end of a shift, they were unable to stand up straight. Many workers who spent years using the short-handled hoe became permanently stooped and suffered from lifelong back pain. Another

The short-handled hoe, or "el cortito," was a tool that was especially hated by farm workers. It was finally banned in 1973.

A worker sprays pesticides on grape vines.

tool, the beethook, which had a razor-sharp blade with a hook attached to the end of it, was used for harvesting beets. Workers used it to pick up beets from the ground and slice the tops off in one swing. Many beet workers lost fingers using the tool.

Field work was also dangerous because of the pesticides—or poisons—used to kill insects on crops. Sometimes workers handled pesticides themselves, and other times pesticides were sprayed from planes directly onto the crops and onto the workers at the same time. Exposure to pesticides could cause headaches, dizziness, and nausea.

LIVING CONDITIONS

Because one of the ways growers made a profit on their crops was to pay migrant workers very low wages, it was difficult for the workers to make enough money to live on. Sometimes every member of a family had to work in order for the family to survive. Children as young as four or five worked in the fields helping their parents.

Because they had so little money, migrant workers often could not afford their own housing. Instead, they lived in sometimes terrible conditions in housing provided on the farms where

A migrant worker's home in California in 1937

they worked. For example, up to four families might live in a one-room shack with no running water or electricity.

Some of the farmers who housed workers on their land subtracted rent money from the workers' wages or made workers pay for transportation to and from the fields. As a result, the workers had little money left over, so it was difficult for them to save enough money to live elsewhere.

In some farm housing, there were no bathing facilities or safe drinking water. Disease was common and would spread quickly in the overcrowded housing. When workers were sick, they often did not get good medical care because they were afraid of losing their jobs if they took time off to seek medical attention. Also, workers who wanted care often didn't have transportation to the doctor's office or hospital or, because they didn't speak English, a way to communicate with health-care workers.

Most children worked in the fields with their parents each day before and after school.

EDUCATION

Because children of migrant workers often worked in the fields alongside their families, many of them did not go to school. Those who did go to school changed schools as often as every few weeks, as their families moved from place to place in search of work. It was hard for them to understand their teachers or participate in their classes because they often spoke little or no English. If they spoke their native languages in school, they risked being bullied by other children or punished by their teachers. Because children who went to school often worked in the fields before and after school, they had little time or energy to study. Therefore, many migrant children didn't do well in school. Not surprisingly, many stopped going to school at a young age and went to work in the fields full time.

3

TIME FOR A CHANGE

UNIONIZATION

It was difficult for migrant workers to try to improve their working and living conditions without a labor union to represent them. Labor unions protect workers' rights by making agreements with employers on behalf of all the workers. These agreements, or contracts, ensure that the rules of working are fair and that all workers are treated equally. Because migrant workers didn't have a labor union, they didn't have contracts with their employers, and so they did not receive fair pay, have job security (meaning they could lose their jobs at any time), or have benefits like health insurance or paid time off.

Since the 1940s, attempts to organize labor unions for farm workers had always failed. Migrant workers didn't stay in one place long enough to have the chance to get to know one another or to team up against the growers themselves. At the same time, the workers didn't trust the people who wanted to help them organize unions. Because the workers were mostly Mexican American and the union organizers were not, the workers felt that the organizers were outsiders. The few workers who did join unions were bullied or fired by the farmers.

UNIONS AND CONTRACTS

A labor union is an organization that is formed to protect workers' rights. Members pay a small amount of money to the union, and, in return, the union takes care of them. Union staff, called *organizers,* draw up contracts with the employers. These contracts set out the rules of working—for example, the hours of work, pay, coffee breaks, and vacations. Union contracts also include general conditions, such as which tools and machinery can be used by the workers, and what employers must do to ensure workers' health and safety.

Employers can't fire members of a union or change their pay without talking to the union first. If there is a **strike**, the union pays workers or provides food and clothing for their families if they need it. If a union member has been unfairly treated at work, the union tries to find a solution with the employer. A union helps workers to stand together, which gives them more power.

CÉSAR CHÁVEZ AND DOLORES HUERTA

One man, César Chávez, was determined to help farm workers stand up for their rights. Chávez was born in Yuma, Arizona, in 1927. In the 1930s, his family moved to California, where, like other migrant worker families, they moved from place to place in search of work. Young César Chávez went to dozens of different schools and was often treated badly by teachers and other students. No matter how difficult their lives were, though, Chávez's father always stood up for his family.

In 1942, Chávez's father was badly injured in a car accident and was unable to work. To help the family, 15-year-old Chávez left school and went to work in the fields full time. During the years he spent as a farm worker, Chávez learned firsthand about the **injustices** the workers faced. He became more and more determined to help change the lives of farm workers for the better. In the early 1950s, he left farm work to fight for workers' rights.

In 1952, Chávez became an organizer for the Community Service Organization, a group in San Jose, California, that helped Mexican migrant workers improve their working and living conditions. The organization helped people with things like filling out forms in English, registering to vote, and enrolling their children in school. Through his work with the Community Service Organization, he got to know a woman named Dolores Huerta.

Like Chávez, Huerta was Mexican American. She was born in Dawson, New Mexico, in 1930. When she was three, she moved with her mother and two brothers to California. Her mother worked two jobs to support her children. When Huerta was 20, she

Dolores Huerta

began training to be a teacher. She went to work in an elementary school but left soon afterward. "I couldn't stand seeing kids come to class hungry and needing shoes," she said later. "I thought I could do more by organizing farm workers than by trying to teach their hungry children." *

After she left teaching, Huerta looked for ways to help set up health and education programs for struggling workers and their families. In 1955, she started an office of the Community Service Organization in Stockton, California. In

César Chávez's family

* http://www.digitalhistory.uh.edu/. Section on Dolores Huerta (the source quoted is the Proclamation of the Delano Grape Workers for International Boycott Day, May 10, 1969).

1960, Huerta began working with a labor union called the Agricultural Workers Organizing Committee (AWOC). The union was trying to help farm workers and their families in Northern California. Huerta wasn't happy working with the AWOC because she didn't think the leaders, who had never lived the life of migrant workers, really understood the workers.

At around the same time, Chávez was beginning to realize that the best way to make a real change for farm workers was to get them to organize their own labor union. When Huerta heard Chávez's plan, she was excited and wanted to be part of it. She decided to leave the AWOC and work with him to create a new union.

A NEW UNION

Chávez and Huerta made a good team. He was quiet and shy, and she was bold and outgoing. Chávez had spent many years working in the fields, so he understood the workers. Huerta had a formal education and was a confident public speaker, so she could work well with government officials and with other union organizers. In 1962, they set up their own union, the National Farm Workers Association, in the city of Delano in California's Central Valley.

Over the next three years, Chávez and Huerta traveled around California trying to get migrant workers to join the union. At first, they struggled to find new members. Most workers didn't believe a union could make a difference in their lives. They had seen workers who joined unions lose their jobs. But Chávez and Huerta were very determined, and they got along with all kinds of people. Workers came to trust Chávez and Huerta because they were Mexican American, like the workers themselves. More and more workers joined the union.

4
THE GREAT DELANO GRAPE STRIKE

TO JOIN OR NOT TO JOIN

In September 1965, the National Farm Workers Association, Chávez and Huerta's union, faced its first major challenge. Filipino workers from grape vineyards in Delano went on strike. Grapes are one of the Central Valley's biggest and most important crops, and the grape harvest requires thousands of workers. That year, Filipino workers who belonged to the AWOC had their hourly wage for grape-picking lowered from $1.40 to $1.00, making their pay lower than the braceros'.

Chávez and Huerta had to decide whether their union would join the AWOC in the grape strike. There were many

Grapes growing in vineyards in California

reasons for the National Farm Workers not to join the strike. For one thing, the AWOC was a rival union. Huerta had worked with the AWOC in the past and had been concerned that its organizers didn't really understand the workers. For another thing, Chávez and Huerta knew that the workers themselves might not want to strike in support of the AWOC. Many of them had seen growers retaliate against strikers in the past and were afraid of losing their jobs. Also, most members of the AWOC were Filipino, and Filipino and Mexican American farm workers had always lived and worked separately.

The strike was risky for the National Farm Workers Association because the union was vulnerable. It was new, still small, and not well-known, and it had relatively few members. The union did not have enough money to support its members during a strike. If the union went on strike and the growers were able to find other workers willing to work in those conditions, it would likely be the end of the union.

Mexican American grape pickers vote to go on strike in Delano, California.

There were also good reasons for the National Farm Workers Association to join the strike. Chávez and Huerta knew that, since grapes were such an important crop, the strike might get national attention. Therefore, being part of the strike would be a way to get more recognition, and hopefully more members, for the National Farm Workers Association. They hoped that publicity from the strike would help people all over the country learn about the struggles of farm workers.

Chávez hoped that striking would build strength and unity within the union, but more than that, he hoped it would build strength and unity among all the farm workers, not just the Filipinos or the Mexican Americans. He believed the grape strike could be more than just a strike. He wanted to turn it into a movement that would lead to big, lasting changes for all farm workers.

A week after the Filipino workers from the AWOC went on strike, Chávez called a meeting of the National Farm Workers Association so the members could vote on whether or not to join the strike. The meeting was packed, and crowds spilled onto the street. He told the workers they were taking part in a struggle for **justice** for all farm workers, not just Mexican

An illustration of a picket during the Great Delano Grape Strike

American ones. He said that it must be a peaceful struggle, even if the growers used violence against the workers. Although Chávez was soft-spoken, people were **inspired** by his words. The meeting ended with thunderous cheers as the National Farm Workers Association voted to go on strike in support of the Filipinos and their union.

The following week, the National Farm Workers Association joined the Filipinos on the picket lines. Filipinos and Mexican Americans were working together for the first time. The strike became known as the Great Delano Grape Strike.

GATHERING SUPPORT

The farm workers' struggle became known as *la causa*, or the cause. It wasn't just a strike for higher wages for grape pickers. Chávez wanted to talk about all of the workers' rights and conditions with the growers. He wanted contracts to be signed between the growers and workers. More than anything, he wanted farm workers to be treated like human beings.

Chávez knew that, for the strike to be successful, the National Farm Workers Association would need help from other workers and other organizations. Otherwise, the grape growers would bring in replacement workers and the strike would fail. During the fall of 1965, Chávez, Huerta, and their staff traveled around California asking more migrant workers to join the union and go on strike.

Chávez and Huerta also asked for help from people who had been involved in the **Civil Rights Movement**. The Civil Rights Movement in the 1950s and '60s helped convince the U.S. government to pass a law guaranteeing people equal rights regardless of their race or sex. People who had worked in the Civil Rights Movement were good at organizing and encouraging people to get involved. They helped to bring publicity and money to la causa.

THE STRIKE SPREADS

At first, the growers ignored the strike. Workers had gone on strike before and had not achieved much. However, the

growers didn't realize how much support Chávez and Huerta would be able to gather. As vineyard workers outside Delano started to hear about Chávez and Huerta and the work they were doing, the strike spread to more vineyards across California.

The growers, realizing they would lose a lot of money if the grapes weren't picked quickly, decided to bring in workers from Mexico to do the picking. However, when the workers from Mexico realized they were breaking a strike, many threw down their tools and joined the picket lines.

News of the strike appeared in newspapers and on TV. News stories showed the growers and the police with their guns and guard dogs, while the men, women, and children on the picket lines stood quietly, carrying signs and union flags. By early October 1965, food and money for the strikers began to arrive from all over the country. Hundreds of people came to Delano to stand on the picket lines with the strikers. The determination of Chávez and Huerta inspired everyone. No matter how impossible things seemed, Chávez said, "Sí, se puede," meaning, "Yes, it can be done."

STRIKES AND PICKET LINES

A strike is one way that workers can protest against something they think is unfair at work. They may want more money or shorter working days. In a strike, the workers stop working, and they don't get paid. A strike is based on the idea that when work stops, the employer loses money because there are no products to sell. The employer may then want to come to an agreement to get the workers back to work. The workers don't always get what they want in a strike.

Picketers often carry signs that tell people what a strike is about.

A picket or a boycott may be used by a union to draw attention to a strike. Workers picket by gathering in a line outside a workplace and trying to convince other workers not to go in. If workers do go in, they are said to have "crossed the picket line." Members of the public sometimes support workers during a strike by not crossing or by joining the picket line.

In a boycott, workers ask the public not to buy an employer's or a group of employers' products. If a boycott is successful, it's because employers aren't making money selling their products, so they settle with the workers to stop the boycott.

5 A LONG, HARD ROAD

HARD TIMES ON THE PICKET LINES

At the beginning of the strike, there were only about 200 picketers, not enough to picket the dozens of entrances to the growers' huge farms. Union organizers handled this problem by using "roving pickets"—moving the picket lines to wherever they would do the most good. When they found out a grower was hiring replacement workers, they set up a peaceful picket line wherever the replacement workers were entering the farm.

As the strike went on, there was more support for the workers, but striking and picketing were still difficult and sometimes dangerous. The growers tried to **intimidate** the strikers. Some

farm bosses raced their pickup trucks up and down the picket lines, throwing clouds of dust onto the workers. Others harassed the picketers by yelling at them or spraying them with pesticide. The growers wanted the strikers to fight back so the police would have an excuse to arrest them.

The striking workers refused to fight back. They were committed to César Chávez's policy of nonviolence. The union held weekly meetings to help keep the workers' spirits up. Instead of responding to the growers' tactics with violence, the picketers sang songs and chanted union slogans, like "Sí, Se Puede!" Even so, many police officers

Strikers form a picket on the grape fields. (Huelga means "strike.")

sided with the growers and arrested picketers for "disturbing the peace."

Though it was difficult, the National Farm Workers Association kept the pickets going all through that winter and into early 1966. Huerta led and organized the picketers. They were often women and children who stood all day at the vineyards while the men tried to get other kinds of work. The sense of pulling together for a shared cause and the growing support of the public helped the strikers and their families stay strong, despite the lack of money and the bullying by the growers. They continued to be inspired by Chávez's determination and Huerta's enthusiasm.

THE MARCH ON SACRAMENTO

Weeks went by, and the growers still refused to recognize or negotiate with the union. In response, Chávez decided

Grape pickers march along the road from Delano to Sacramento.

to do something dramatic to draw more attention to the strike. He and his followers decided to organize a march to the state capital, Sacramento. Chávez called it a *peregrinación*, or **pilgrimage**.

The march left Delano in mid March of 1966. Hundreds of people joined the protesters as they walked the 300 miles north. TV crews followed them as they held parties and **rallies** in towns and villages along the way. Each time they stopped, they read out the Plan of Delano *(see Appendix A, page 31)*.

A few days before the marchers arrived in Sacramento, one of the growers agreed to recognize the union, which meant they considered the union a legal representative of the workers. The grower, Schenley Industries, was one of the biggest in the Delano area. Dolores Huerta drew up a contract with Schenley. The company agreed to give workers a pay raise of 35 cents an hour and to use "hiring halls."

Some of the smaller growers realized that, sooner or later, they would have to

THE MARCH ON SACRAMENTO

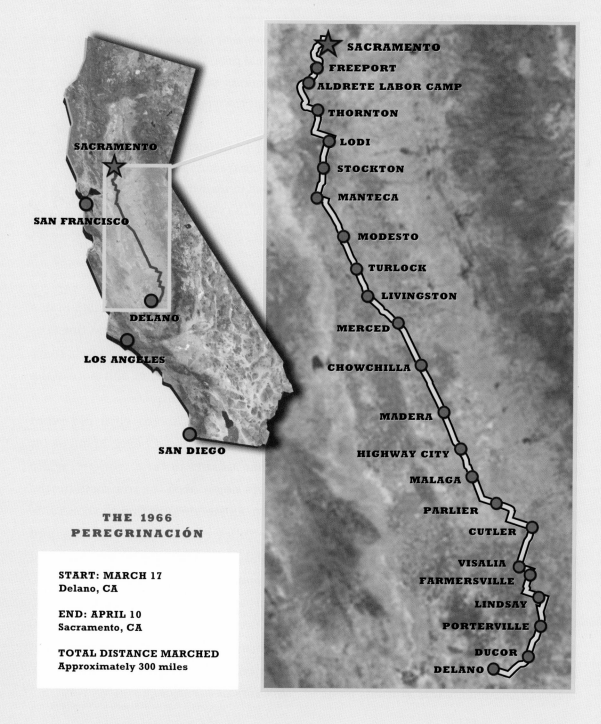

SACRAMENTO

SACRAMENTO
FREEPORT
ALDRETE LABOR CAMP
THORNTON
LODI
STOCKTON
MANTECA
MODESTO
TURLOCK
LIVINGSTON
MERCED
CHOWCHILLA
MADERA
HIGHWAY CITY
MALAGA
PARLIER
CUTLER
VISALIA
FARMERSVILLE
LINDSAY
PORTERVILLE
DUCOR
DELANO

SAN FRANCISCO

DELANO

LOS ANGELES

SAN DIEGO

THE 1966
PEREGRINACIÓN

START: MARCH 17
Delano, CA

END: APRIL 10
Sacramento, CA

TOTAL DISTANCE MARCHED
Approximately 300 miles

HIRING HALLS

A hiring hall is an office, usually run by a union, that matches up workers with growers and protects workers at the same time. Through the hiring hall, the union provides an employer with workers who have the right skills for a job. The union also makes sure that the employer is providing fair pay and safe working conditions.

Before the hiring halls, farm workers got jobs through labor contractors hired by the growers. Because the labor contractors made money by taking a percentage of the workers' pay, it was in their interest to get as many workers hired as possible, regardless of the workers' pay or working conditions.

recognize the union, too. They also realized that if they paid lower wages than Schenley, there would be more strikes and boycotts, and they would lose money.

On Easter Sunday, 1966, 25 days after the march had begun, the pilgrims hobbled into Sacramento. They were **jubilant**. Chávez had been right when he said "It can be done." The march was a victory for the union, but real and lasting change would not happen until more growers agreed to sign contracts.

THE UNITED FARM WORKERS OF AMERICA

Though the National Farm Workers Association still had a long way to go, the march to Sacramento was a turning point. It made people all over the United States notice farm workers for the first time. Because of the strike and the march, more workers joined the union, and more of the growers signed contracts.

Chávez and Huerta each did what they were best at. Chávez spent a lot of time talking to farm workers, while Huerta **negotiated** the contracts for the union. She made sure that the contracts were followed, set up hiring halls, and helped hundreds of workers who had complaints against their employers.

In 1967, the National Farm Workers Association joined with the AWOC to form a bigger, stronger union that later became known as the United Farm Workers of America.

6

THE GREAT GRAPE BOYCOTT

IN THE SUMMER of 1967, the new union decided to focus its efforts on growers of table grapes, or eating grapes. The Great Delano Grape Strike had been against growers who grew grapes used for making wine.

In the middle of the harvest that August, thousands of workers at the Giumarra Corporation went on strike to protest low wages. Giumarra was California's largest table-grape grower. Workers at other vineyards soon followed. The growers were desperate to get the fruit picked, so they brought in workers who were not part of the union.

Because the union couldn't stop the grapes from being picked, Chávez decided to try to stop Giumarra from selling them. He asked people across the country to **boycott**, or stop buying, table grapes grown by Giumarra. Giumarra tried to fool shoppers by putting the labels of other growers on its grapes. Chávez responded by asking the public to stop buying all California grapes.

The Giumarra boycott grew into the famous Great Grape Boycott, which began in January 1968. Chávez sent organizers all over the United States to talk to people and encourage them to stop buying grapes. Once the public learned about the difficult lives of farm workers, they were happy to stop buying grapes in order to support the workers.

Supporters of the boycott across the country respected that the strikers never used violence.

KEEPING THE PEACE

Meanwhile, the Great Delano Grape Strike was still going on. Growers began using violent **tactics** against the strikers. It was becoming harder and harder for Chávez to keep the strikers under control and to keep the union's promise of non-violence. In February of 1968, to remind the workers of their promise, he decided to go on a **fast**, or to stop eating.

At first, people didn't understand what Chávez was doing, but his fast was very

PICKING GRAPES

Grape workers were paid according to how many grapes they picked. Wine grapes could be picked quickly because workers could throw them in a bin knowing they would be crushed later. Table grapes had to be picked more carefully, which meant that it took longer to pick table grapes than wine grapes. Table grape workers thought it was unfair that the slower picking made their wages lower than those of other grape workers.

Migrant workers pick wine grapes.

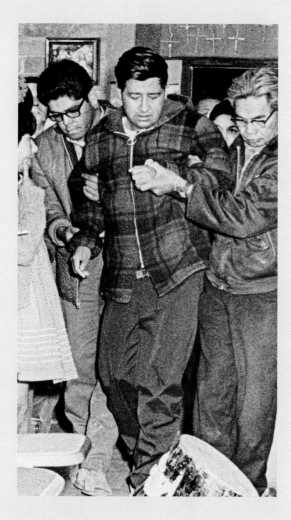

(Left) Supporters help Chávez walk to a meeting four days before he ends his fast.

(Above) Chávez and John Giumarra, Jr., from the Giumarra Corporation celebrate the signing of the contract.

effective. It attracted a lot of attention from the media, and it united the strikers. Chávez fasted for 25 days and lost more than 30 pounds in weight. The fast got Chávez's message across to the workers and the public: The union was committed to nonviolence.

The Great Grape Boycott continued for two years. The workers never gave up. Finally, in July of 1970, the Giumarra Corporation signed a contract that gave workers pay raises. Giumarra also provided fresh water and toilets in the fields, medical plans, and protection against pesticides. Other growers soon followed its example.

7

NEW BATTLES,
NEW VICTORIES

DURING THE 1970s, the United Farm Workers of America continued to improve the working and living conditions of farm workers using the same nonviolent methods. Growers had to accept that times were changing. By 1980, thousands of migrant workers had contracts that gave them better pay, paid vacations, health plans, and some guarantees for safe working conditions. The short-handled hoe was eventually completely banned. Although there were still thousands of workers who traveled around following the harvest, most now had a home to go to at the end of the season. Many could earn enough money so their children didn't have to work in the fields and could go to school.

THE CAMPAIGN AGAINST PESTICIDES

Well into the 1980s, most growers sprayed their crops with pesticides. Some even continued to spray pesticides from airplanes while workers were in the fields. The workers were being poisoned by being exposed to pesticides on the crops they handled and in the air they breathed. In 1983, health workers documented that many farm workers were getting cancer.

In 1984, Chávez and the United Farm

Crops are often sprayed with pesticides from airplanes.

Workers of America started a new boycott, focused on the use of pesticides. Organizers from the union helped inform the public that the produce they were buying and eating had been treated with chemicals that made farm workers sick. Shoppers began to refuse to buy grapes and other crops that had been sprayed with dangerous pesticides. In 1988, Chávez fasted for 36 days to try to change California's law. Thanks in part

to the efforts of Chávez and the United Farm Workers of America, California now has strict rules on the use of pesticides.

THE STRUGGLE GOES ON

César Chávez died in 1993, at age 66. In 1994, President Bill Clinton awarded him the U.S. Medal of Freedom. At the award ceremony, the President said, "This remarkable man . . . led a very courageous life. And in so doing, he brought

Chávez protests against grapes that are sprayed with pesticides.

dignity to the lives of so many others and provided for us inspiration for the rest of our nation's history."

Dolores Huerta continues to work for the rights of migrant workers and Mexican Americans. She has helped to get **unemployment benefits**, medical plans, and even homes for farm workers. In 2002, she received the Puffin Foundation/National Institute Award for Creative Citizenship.

Farm laborers still work long hours for low wages, but, thanks to the work of Chávez and Huerta and the United Farm Workers of America, they are protected by laws that guarantee safe working conditions and fair pay. Some employers still look for ways to get around the laws, but the United Farm Workers of America will always be there to fight for justice for the workers.

THE PLAN OF DELANO

The Plan of Delano was published in the *El Macriado* newspaper on March 17, 1966. It was read aloud at every stop on the pilgrimage to Sacramento and was an inspiration for Chávez's followers. These are its main points:

1. We seek our basic, God-given rights as human beings. Because we have suffered—and are not afraid to suffer—in order to survive, we are ready to give up everything, even our lives, in our fight for social justice. We shall do it without violence because that is our **destiny**.
2. We seek the support of all political groups and protection of the government, which is also our government, in our struggle. For too many years we have been treated as the lowest of the low. WE SHALL BE HEARD.
3. We seek and have the support of the Church in what we do. GOD SHALL NOT ABANDON US.
4. We are suffering. We have suffered and are not afraid to suffer in order to win our cause. We draw our strength from the very **despair** in which we have been forced to live. WE SHALL ENDURE.
5. We shall unite. We know why these United States are just that—united. The strength of the poor is also in union. UNITED WE SHALL STAND.
6. We will strike. We are sons of the Mexican Revolution, a revolution of the poor seeking bread and justice. We want to be equal with all the working men in the nation; we want a just wage, better working conditions, a decent future for our children. To those who oppose us, be they ranchers, police, politicians, or **speculators**, we say that we are going to continue fighting until we die, or we win. WE SHALL OVERCOME.

History is on our side.
May the strike go on!

TIMELINE OF EVENTS

1927	▪ César Chávez born in Yuma, Arizona
1930	▪ Dolores Huerta born in Dawson, New Mexico
1929	▪ The Great Depression begins
1942	▪ Chávez leaves school and begins working in the fields full time
	▪ Bracero Program set up
1945	▪ World War II ends
1952	▪ Chávez begins working for a community organization that supports Mexican Americans
1960	▪ Huerta begins working for the Agricultural Workers Organizing Committee
1962	▪ Chávez moves to Delano and forms the National Farm Workers Association
1964	▪ Civil Rights Act passed
1965	▪ September, the Great Delano Grape Strike begins
	▪ Chávez and Huerta travel around California asking for help with the strike
1966	▪ March 17, pilgrimage to Sacramento begins
	▪ April 10, pilgrimage arrives in Sacramento
	▪ Boycott and support spreads across the United States
	▪ Some growers sign agreements
1967	▪ NFWA merges with AWOC and becomes United Farm Workers of America
	▪ August, grape workers go on strike
1968	▪ January, boycott of all Californian table grapes begins
	▪ February, Chávez starts 25-day fast
1970	▪ July, contract signed with the Giumarra Corporation

1978	▪	Grape boycotts end
1983	▪	Health workers noticed that farm workers have high rates of cancer
1984	▪	New grape boycott against pesticides
1988	▪	Chávez fasts for 36 days against pesticide use
1993	▪	April 23, Chávez dies
1994	▪	Chávez awarded U.S. Medal of Freedom by President Clinton
2002	▪	Huerta awarded the Puffin Foundation/National Institute Award for Creative Citizenship

GLOSSARY

BOYCOTT: to refuse to have anything to do with something—for example, to refuse to buy a product because you're not happy with the way it's made

CIVIL RIGHTS MOVEMENT: a movement during the 1950s and '60s when people protested against the way African Americans were treated

DEPORTATION: sending someone out of a country

DESPAIR: a feeling of hopelessness

DESTINY: the events that happen to a person in the future

EXPLOITED: when a person or situation is used in an unfair or selfish way; taken advantage of

FAST: to go without food

FERTILE: land that can grow any crops

FILIPINO: a person from the Philippines

GENERATION: a period of time during which people are born, grow up, become adults, and have children of their own

ILLEGALLY: against the law

INJUSTICE: action or treatment that is unfair

INSPIRED: excited and motivated

INTIMIDATE: to frighten a person in order to make him or her do something

JUBILANT: thrilled or joyful

JUSTICE: fairness

NEGOTIATED: reached agreement about something by talking about it

PILGRIMAGE: a journey for a specific reason

PRODUCE: things that have been made or grown, especially by farming

RALLY: a large meeting of people showing support for something

SEARING: extremely hot

SPECULATOR: a person who buys and sells land to make money

STRIKE: when people refuse to work until their demands are met in order to make their lives better

TACTIC: an action that is planned to achieve something

UNEMPLOYMENT BENEFITS: pay for workers who are unable to find work

BIBLIOGRAPHY

Roger Bruns: *César Chávez: A Biography* (Greenwood Press, 2005)

César Chávez (ed. Jensen and Hammerback): *The Words of César Chávez* (Texas A & M Univ. Press, 2002)

John Gregory Dunne: *Delano, The Story of the California Grape Strike* (Farrer, Strauss and Giroux, 1967)

Susan Ferriss and Ricardo Sandoval (ed. Diana Hembree): *The Fight in the Fields: César Chávez and the Farmworkers Movement* (Harcourt Brace, 1997)

Peter Matthiessen: *Sal Si Puedes: César Chávez and the New American Revolution* (Random House, 1969)

INDEX